HOW TO STOP MASTURBATION:

Ultimate guide on how to control your thoughts and stop masturbation

Richard H. Jacobs

TABLE OF CONTENT

AUDIENCE

This book is meant for everyone who is into the habit of masturbation and wish to control it to a stop. But special attention is paid to teens and adult as they are the most people who engaged in masturbation. I recommend you to read this book irrespective of age as the techniques and steps outline will give the same results for all age grades

Chapter 1

What is masturbation?

There's an old joke about masturbation: "80% of people masturbate, and the other 20% are lying about it." This isn't a genuine number, of course (because some individuals actually don't ever masturbate). But it does come to the point where most people realize masturbation is frequent and natural — even if they don't confess to doing it themselves.

Some individuals are uncomfortable about masturbating since there are a number of stereotypes out there that masturbation is nasty or embarrassing. It may appear like nobody does it, since masturbating is private and people normally don't speak about it.

But the honest reality is most people masturbate. Men masturbate. Women masturbate. Trans and genderqueer persons masturbate. Straight people, homosexual individuals, and bisexual people masturbate. People of all ages masturbate. Others folks masturbate a few times a day, some just do it every once in awhile. And other individuals never masturbate – that's absolutely acceptable, too. Masturbating is a personal choice; only do it if you want to.

Many people assume that masturbation is solely for single people or individuals who aren't having sex, but that's not true at all. Lots of individuals masturbate no matter what their relationship situation is, for lots of varied reasons. It's entirely natural if your girlfriend or boyfriend masturbates (or wants to masturbate) - it doesn't mean you're not good enough, and it doesn't indicate they're not into you.

Can you masturbate too much?
A lot of people worry about masturbating "too much," yet it's entirely good to masturbate a lot — even more than once a day.

Masturbating is only an issue if it comes in the way of attending to school, work, hanging out with your friends and family, and doing other things you enjoy. But as long as masturbation doesn't get in the way of your normal life, you don't have to worry about doing it too often. Masturbating on the regular is perfectly fine.

What should I do if someone discovers me masturbating?
Masturbating is private, and it may be humiliating when someone catches you. But you know what? Chances are, they've masturbated too. So they probably know

how you're feeling and understand your humiliation.

If someone comes in on you masturbating, you may laugh it off or make a joke to help make it less embarrassing. It's also definitely a good opportunity to chat with them about privacy and personal space. Everyone deserves to feel comfortable examining their own body in privacy.

Masturbating takes up a lot of your time and energy
Your home, job, or personal life is suffering because of masturbating
You could be late to meetings, cancel activities, or leave social appointments early to masturbate\sYou masturbate in public or in uncomfortable situations because you can't wait to go home
You masturbate even when you don't feel aroused, sexual, or "horny"

When you sense unpleasant emotions—such as anger, worry, tension, or sadness—your go-to reaction is to masturbate for consolation
You feel guilty, worried, or unhappy after masturbating
You masturbate even if you don't want to\sYou find it difficult to quit thinking about masturbation
Any one of these symptoms might be significant, but if you're having many concerns, that's an indication of a broader problem.

Negative Impacts of Excessive Masturbation
Excessive masturbation may lead toward a range of difficulties, both personal and interpersonal, that create physical, emotional, and social suffering. There is sometimes a steady trend toward excess, and many who find themselves suffering genuinely wish to quit. Masturbation to this level is usually combined with other life

concerns or diagnosable mental health and/or addiction disorders. 3

Excessive, obsessive, or chronic masturbating may create harmful repercussions like:

Skin irritation
Edema (swelling) (swelling)
Inability to connect with a sexual partner
Social isolation\sExcessive reading of pornographic content\sFailure to properly fulfill major life activities (e.g., parenting, working, going to school) (e.g., parenting, working, going to school)
Disinterest in activities formerly enjoyed\sStress
Lowered self-esteem
Feelings of guilt or shame\sDepression, anxiety, and other mental health difficulties
Potential to acquire infection or physically damaged from incorrect use and maintenance of sex toys\sPotential for legal troubles if caught masturbating in public

and other banned places\sPotential for masturbation addiction
Said affects are not by any means all-inclusive and do vary by kind and severity per individual.

Chapter 2

How to stop masturbation

15 Tips for How to Stop Masturbating Fortunately, there are several techniques to regulate desires. Some may work better than others, but the most critical aspect is desire to change. Oftentimes, the bigger number of methods you go about working through the issue, the higher possibility that the desired change will occur.

Here are 15 guidelines if you wish to quit masturbating—while not complete, it should offer you some ideas for where to start:

1. Talk About It With Your Romantic Partner or Others You Trust

It might help to discuss freely about a problem with masturbating with a love partner or someone else you trust. These folks may give emotional support while helping you measure your development. Although the issue is forbidden in many circumstances and hard to speak about, it is probable that everyone you choose to talk to presently masturbates or has done so in the past. No longer feeling alone may be a relief in-and-of itself.

With love relationships, it is crucial to be on the same page. Physical closeness, whatever it looks like, is a crucial element of every relationship. Perhaps something is absent in the connection. In other circumstances, it may be a problem of performance anxiety or other unpleasant thoughts and feelings. Whatever the situation, addressing the fundamental reason is frequently the first step to achieving change. Whether individually or as couples, sex therapy may be useful in moving ahead.

2. Focus on Your Partner(s) (s)

Intimacy is a vital aspect of every love connection. What it looks like varies greatly, but mutual exploration is beneficial. Honestly discuss together, or among partners, what each of your preferences, wants, and requirements are. Next, negotiate what works. From there, build upon the usual pattern by doing more of what each of you love and/or even attempting new things. This is connecting, pleasant, healthy, and distracts from masturbating.

3. Limit Time Alone

Although masturbation is an activity that may be done in couples or groups, it is typically done in solitary. The more time alone, the more opportunity you have to masturbate. Limiting time alone restricts these options.

4. Stop Watching Porn

It is usual for masturbation to occur while viewing pornography, so if that's the case for you, it's time to quit watching porn. The strength of pornography is that it activates the pleasure pathway as one pleasures in a blend of imagination and a naturally occurring high. 4 Though discussing openly about pornography is usually considered taboo as well, current figures suggest a significant demand for pornographic material, particularly online (which could be a problem in your relationship[s], especially if your spouse considers porn unfaithful) (which might be an issue in your relationship[s], especially if your partner considers porn cheating).

Here are some current data concerning porn consumption and addiction:

5

About 200,000 Americans are labeled as "porn addicts"
40 million American individuals routinely access porn sites

35% of all internet downloads are connected to pornography

Ways to quit viewing porn may include setting blockers on explicit websites, purposefully avoiding them, and being online in public locations where such conduct is outlawed. Elevated watching and participation in pornographic material, among other things, may also put you at increased risk for porn addiction.

5. Change Up the Routine

Although masturbation may be spontaneous, it frequently happens at regular times of the day. These may include when you wake up, take a shower, arrive home from school or work, before bed, or anytime else has become habitual. If this is true, it may help to try something different. If a lengthy hot shower is one of these moments, consider having a fast, cold shower. If the time is first thing in the morning, get out of bed with the alarm and begin with whatever follows next in the routine—perhaps a nutritious meal. If it is before to bed, do something more calming like listening to peaceful music with your eyes closed.

6. Limit Accessibility to Sex Toys

Sex toys may be triggering. Seeing them is a reminder of a "better" time you might be experiencing. Such temptation may gradually drive toward a return to previous habit, therefore eliminating them is still another strategy to develop your relapse prevention plan and reduce your reminders.

7. Meditate

Meditation is a highly powerful practice that has multiple evidence-based benefits. Its potential to cultivate the mind-body-spirit pathway is vast, and it may be useful in stopping masturbation as well. Focusing on something good such as a mantra or joyful idea while taking purposely deep breaths will shift your thoughts. During this period, desires may diminish. Once done, it becomes easy to concentrate on anything else.

8. Utilize Unstimulating Visualizations

Masturbation is sometimes done while contemplating something that heightens excitement. Rather than concentrating on something exciting, try something that accomplishes the reverse. For example, instead of thinking on someone you believe to be beautiful, imagine someone or something that is opposite of your taste. Whatever the vision, the crucial thing is that it be something that distracts from, rather than incites, a desire to masturbate.

9. Implement Healthy Distractions

Healthy diversions may be anything: Reading a book, writing a diary entry, playing a board game, gardening, and so on are all healthy hobbies that interest you on several levels. Even less healthful hobbies such as streaming media or playing video games are totally appropriate in moderation. Socially, this may mean getting out with friends, making a phonecall, sending a kind text, or anything else positively engaging people. The trick here is not substituting one unpleasant habit (masturbation) with another.

10. Exercise

Exercise, like meditation, is a multifunctional activity. Notably renowned for its physical health advantages, exercise also promotes mental health. The release of endorphins lowers pain and tension while creating a relaxing effect. Dopamine is also released, which boosts your mood. An extra social advantage might be having your friends present. Whether in the company of others or not, exercise may assist divert and relieve stress from cravings to masturbate. Over time, you may also feel and look better, which promotes self-concept. Win-win-win!

If going to the gym or conventional exercise is unpleasant, that is alright. Exercise may be kept easy by taking walks, cleaning the home, caring to the grass, using stairs instead of elevators, and in so many more ways you may not ordinarily think. If you are in motion, the activity counts. Keep going.

11. Set Goals & Mark Progress
Like everything else, quitting completely can—at first—be apparently impossible. Begin by reducing down the amount of times each day slowly. This may be done daily or weekly, but the idea is for the behavior to reduce to the intended target in a timely timeframe. Setting realistic SMART (specific, measurable, achievable, relevant, and timely) objectives may assist here.

As development happens, confidence will be created. And sure, it does grow easier with time. Setbacks are likely and might be upsetting; but, you are the only one who can eventually get yourself back on track.

12. Look Toward Religion

For people embracing diverse faiths, there are differing ideas towards masturbation. It may be regarded suitable, frowned upon, or absolutely banned. If this is appropriate, it may assist to contemplate regarding masturbation with regards to your faith. This may be done alone, with help from others, or even by conversing with a trustworthy religious leader. If religion is what is contributing toward feelings of guilt among other issues, contact with a mental health expert is suggested if feasible. Culturally competent specialists may help you deal through any pain within the framework of your faith. This is psychologically and spiritually healthy.

13. Wear Extra Clothes at Night

Although wearing more garments at night may be unpleasant or require some fenagling of the thermostat, it offers an additional protective layer. Sleeping naked or in little clothes enhances accessibility.

More layers of clothes allow greater time to deal with desires.

14. Work on Anything Else That Needs Work

While concentrating on lowering or ceasing masturbating, it helps to concentrate on anything else that needs attention. Diverting your attention toward other areas of need decreases the emphasis on masturbation while leading toward overall life improvements. This may entail going to school or interviewing for a new job. Or it may be something social—enhancing meaningful connections with people. All of us have something we would want to better. Whatever it is, establish a healthy objective around it and continue accordingly.

15. Speak With a Professional

With practically any problem, dealing with an expert in that particular subject is recommended. In this scenario, consulting with a counselor or addiction expert is an excellent start. Licensed professional therapists are required by HIPAA to safeguard confidentially (with specific constraints) and have dealt with others who have similar concerns. They have the expertise, experience, and skills to assist you work through the challenge. It is possible that there are internalized issues with negative thoughts and feelings such as worry, despair, and shame. These are normal and can be helped.

If patients feel that they masturbate too often and do not know how to stop masturbating, here is a way out. Porn addiction and masturbation go hand in hand, and they have become a major problem that millions of people all across the globe across all ages and both sexes suffer from. A lot of individuals are hooked to masturbation, and they are continuously asking how to quit masturbating since they frequently detest themselves after this process of too much masturbation.

The impulse to masturbate is a normal one, particularly in youth, since it signals interest in sex before beginning on adult sexual relationships. Masturbation is a shortcut to acquire the natural enjoyment that comes with reproduction, but when it becomes an obsession or a cause for persistent self-loathing, then maybe it is time to discover how to quit masturbation addiction. Read along further to learn how to stop masturbating, what are the anti-masturbation drugs and treatments used to conquer this addiction, and how to get professional assistance.

How To Stop Masturbation Addiction On Your Own?
Perhaps the most prevalent difficulty with masturbation addiction, particularly in married couples, is how it impacts one's connection with the spouse. They quickly start to feel unloved, inadequate, and dissatisfied. The following tackles how to

quit masturbation, and it does not concentrate on concerns such as why individuals desire to stop masturbating or whether or not it is healthy.

There are so many ways to confront the masturbation problem, but they are all very likely to fall under one of a few categories.

One may quit masturbation addiction in a few ways when one contemplates how to stop masturbating; some of these techniques which have been documented in this research are addressed below:

Stop torturing oneself. Remember that masturbation is truly a normal want, and as human beings, individuals constantly have these sexual cravings, and none of these things makes them less of a person or any less deserving compared to anybody. Don't allow oneself to slip into melancholy since this is typically a waste of time, and it might have been spent releasing oneself of the addiction. So take it a step at a time and understand that there is aid; the situation is not hopeless.

Remove the stimuli that provide temptation to masturbate. Top of the list of things that creates the urge to masturbate is pornography, thus one needs to clear oneself and the immediate surroundings of any pornographic material. Also, one should manage access to this stuff. If one is attentive enough to know the particular times and situations, one generally experiences the temptation to masturbate, attempt to be occupied with other things at such moments. Some individuals propose exercising since this delivers a release of its own and leaves a person fatigued to accomplish much else

Reduce the alone time. If one regularly masturbates as a consequence of loneliness, discover measures to reduce alone. Do actions that are generally done alone in the presence of people in public venues. Don't shut oneself up inside all day.

Find another outlet for time and energy. Fill life with intriguing activities. The exhilaration of doing something unusual and reaching specified goals and objectives may help replace the want to masturbate, and there are a lot more distractions that can take one's mind off it. The technique of channeling one's sexual cravings into creative output is something that monks and sages have perfected, and it is called sublimation. This is something one can employ on a scale that one is capable of. There are a variety of activities that one might put time and energy into, such as writing, learning to play an instrument, sketching, etc. This requires discipline and effort, and no one ever claimed it was going to be easy. Research has also revealed that the way one lives may either boost or diminish self-control when it comes to coping with addictions.

Be persistent and patient. Stopping masturbation is not something that can be done instantaneously. It is a process that demands dedication, and one could succumb to temptation and relapse on occasion. Don't beat oneself up when this occurs. One may also build up a reward system to reward oneself for excellent conduct and accomplishment in terms of how long one goes without masturbating. When one maintains a record of how long one has gone without masturbating, the longer the record survives, the harder it is for one to participate in conduct that would damage that record. Doing this gives a fresh motive that may assist one get over the finish line. A drive to maintain a record and pride in how long one has refrained will soon overpower the impulse to masturbate, and at this point, the war against addiction is practically won.

Don't hurry the procedure. Stopping masturbation is not a one-time action. One needs to be patient and give oneself the appropriate time and treatment that is necessary to overcome this addiction.

Adopt a healthy diet and lifestyle. In order to overcome any form of addiction, a healthy diet and lifestyle are highly crucial as it helps one's impulses lessen and also offers incentive to resist.

Wear additional garments at night. Wearing extra garments at night may assist establish a physical barrier and inhibit one from touching oneself. It will lessen the feeling and will help inhibit the impulse to masturbate.

When everything else fails, seek expert assistance. Help may be sought through enrolling in a therapeutic community and therapy. The community might take the shape of support groups, internet forums, and accountability partners. The study demonstrates that professional aid in this area may go a long way in arresting this behavior and avoiding it in the future.

Chapter 3

What are the effects of masturbation?

Most youngsters play with their genitals between the ages of two and six. To a grown-up person, the sight of youngsters fondling their own genitals might seem unsettling since he/she looks at the behavior through adult lenses. However, this behavior is a very typical aspect of growing up for every kid, since it is a process of self-exploring their own bodies and understanding how each area of their body reacts to touch, and how certain sections are more delightful than others. To a youngster stroking his/her genitals just feels naively good and is neither "wrong" or "bad". These "adult filters" are typically given to the youngsters by the adults, and often the kid ends up feeling confused and anxious.

These people respond to the kid in the same manner that they observed their own parents or grown-ups around them react, when they were discovering their own bodies as youngsters. Therefore, they continue to carry those sentiments of guilt and never had an opportunity to grow comfortable with their own sexuality.

The act in itself is neither "good" or "bad", however in certain situations, religious beliefs may encourage individuals to describe it as "bad".

The essential component in such a circumstance would be how an adult approaches a kid and helps the child feel comfortable with his/her own body and gently explains the propriety side of it, should the child participate in the behavior in front of others, but without humiliating the child.

Sexual development is a very much a necessary aspect of normal growth and development for a kid, just as physical development, emotional development, learning and developing language and communication abilities are normal.

Having said that, what also has to be said is, even if there is nothing wrong with masturbating, it is also appropriate not to masturbate. Some individuals have naturally reduced levels of sexual desire or may decide that they wish to refrain from masturbating for religious or personal reasons. You may pursue any choice you believe is best for you.

Is masturbation a common behaviour?
Experts and academics in sexuality believe that masturbation is a totally natural procedure for human beings and is a healthy sexual habit. It probably has a negative reputation since it is an incredibly private sexual practice, which no one discusses even with the closest of friends.

Is masturbating harmful?

No. From a health science standpoint, masturbating is not at all hazardous for you. Some individuals believe masturbation is harmful for moral grounds, but, that is a personal decision.

Is it healthy for a guy to masturbate daily?
There is no proper response to this question. Masturbating everyday might be typical for some guys, however for others it can be excessive. As long as masturbation does not influence your overall energy levels, and does not infringe on your everyday life and activities, you should be alright.

Though, few sex experts consider masturbating everyday to be excessive. Masturbating everyday may lead to weakness, weariness, early ejaculation and may impede sexual activities with your partner.

On the other side, missing out on frequent orgasms raises stress levels and may lead to mental health difficulties, dissatisfaction, and unhappiness in general. Masturbating improves stress release and helps to balance your mood, making you happier and healthier.

How many times in a week is masturbating considered typical for a man?
Again, there is no proper response to this issue since the frequency each week might vary from man to man dependent on his overall health circumstances. There are guys who masturbate two to three times a day, or five times a week, or even once a week.

Sexual urge is normal, but, an excess of anything is detrimental. Therefore, rather of increasing the frequency of masturbation you might try redirecting your energy to activities such as sports, or any other interests. This guarantees that you live a balanced, healthy and happy life.

Can masturbation substitute having sex with a partner for men?

Masturbation has its own place and so does sex with a partner. In reality, masturbation may improve the experience with a sexual partner, since it helps you understand your own body better.

However, if masturbation starts to disrupt sexual life with your partner then it might be an indication of a problem. Due to masturbation, if you miss out on sex with your partner you lose the sensation of intimacy with a spouse.

There are genuine occasions nevertheless when masturbating may substitute sex, for example:

if the partner's sex drive is weaker than yours then masturbation is an alternative
if the spouse is sick\sif your partner is pregnant\sif the partner is not available

Can masturbating cause premature ejaculation?
Excessive masturbation may cause harm to the nerves that allow for the ejaculation. This might induce premature ejaculation or even an ejaculation during sleep.

Don't wait or self medicate.
See a doctor now

Find and schedule an appointment among 100+ physicians in Bangalore:
Can masturbating influence your sperm count?
Masturbation does not alter the amount of sperms you create, since sperms are continually produced in the bodies of men.

It does take time, though, after one ejaculation to ejaculate another. This is totally normal and in no way is an indicator of your sperm count being low.

When is masturbating not safe for men? Masturbation is typically safe. However, if it is done excessively and violently then it might be dangerous.

When you contact the genitals of an infected individual and then touch yours you may suffer from Sexually Transmitted Infections (STIs) (STIs). STIs may also emerge if you share your sex devices with an infected individual.

If you masturbate in a face-down posture you tend to apply greater pressure on the penis, and you may hurt it. To prevent this you may masturbate while standing, sitting, or resting on the back.

You should avoid squeezing the penis when ejaculating, to inhibit the flow of semen. Else, this may harm the nerves and blood vessels in the penis, and will also drive the semen into the urine bladder.

Can masturbating make you thin?

Masturbation does not make you slim. However, excessive masturbation might help you lose a little weight, since theoretically, it is like any activity you conduct.

Will a man's testosterone level fall due to masturbation?
No. Masturbating only has a moderate influence on circulating testosterone as a study demonstrates. However, again moderation is the key. Masturbating excessively will undoubtedly diminish testosterone levels.

What are the advantages of masturbating for men?
Masturbation is a component of healthy sex life and study indicates lots of health advantages for men after masturbation, it is advantageous in the following ways:

For males, masturbating may help avoid prostate cancer. Toxins grow up spontaneously in the urogenital tract. Men who ejaculate over five times each week lower these toxic levels. This dramatically decreases their chance of prostate cancer.

When males ejaculate, a little cortisol is produced, which is the stress hormone. This strengthens their immune system.

Masturbation may alleviate stress and tension from the body by flooding the system with endorphins. Endorphins produce a good mood in the body and may contribute to restful sleep.

With aging males naturally lose muscular tone even in the penis. Masturbation or regular sex in a manner strengthens the pelvic floor muscles and prevent erectile dysfunction and incontinence.

Masturbating generates feel-good neurochemicals like dopamine and oxytocin that improves your spirits, enhances your contentment, and stimulates the reward circuits in your brain.

It might increase your bond with your spouse because you know yourself physically.
Is excessive masturbation damaging to a man's health? Side effects of masturbating
Excess of anything may be hazardous. Masturbating excessively may cause:

fatigue\sweakness
early ejaculation\smay also hinder sexual activities with your partner\sinjury to the penis\svision changes
lower back ache
testicular pain
hair loss
If you find yourself excessively masturbating, you may wish to channel the surplus energy in a more healthful manner, such as :

yoga\smeditation
listening to music

enrolling dancing classes\sfollowing a workout program such as aerobics, jogging, cycling, swimming etc

If the inclination continues, you may wish to contact a psychiatrist or a therapist since it might also be connected to mental stress.

How do I know if I am masturbating excessively?

You know you're masturbating excessively when:

it causes you tremendous anguish.

you are masturbating numerous times per day to escape from stress or reality of day to day living.

you routinely harm yourself by rubbing forcefully.

you scarcely have time for your friends or family since you are too busy pleasuring yourself.

you continually feel lustful and battle the temptation to enjoy yourself.

you get pain in your genitals.

What is the therapy of excessive masturbation?

You immediately need to contact a general doctor, who may, in turn, send you to a psychiatrist or a counselor.

Perhaps India too needs to speak about masturbation more openly?
In the year 2009, the European countries, including the United Kingdom undertook a huge pro-masturbation drive with the purpose of detracting teens from participating in dangerous sexual conduct that might lead to STDs or unplanned pregnancies. Pamphlets were prepared providing essential information regarding masturbation which were given to parents, teens and youth workers. This is a concept worth examining in India. In fact, not simply about masturbation. Perhaps lessons can be attended on complete sexual education which can also include masturbation along with suggestions of how

excessive masturbation can be destructive and advise on how to proactively channel away the surplus sexual energy to highly creative endeavors.

Each year, over 1000 individuals die attempting to strangle themselves while masturbating
This is known as Autoerotic Asphyxiation. When the brain's supply of oxygen is cut off momentarily (asphyxia), a person enjoys a euphoric high seconds before he loses consciousness. There are individuals hooked to this. These Autoerotic asphyxiators seek this high in order to achieve the next degree of sexual ecstasy, and end up strangling themselves with cords, ropes, scarves, and knots. Though weird some even resort to wrapping their heads with plastic bags! Doctors, as well as psychologists seldom speak about this topic since they do not want to place hazardous thoughts in the brains of young and inexperienced individuals. But such a step could be seen as

a double-edged sword, as young people need to be made aware of the dangers they could put themselves in, in their search for pleasurable thrill but it could also give them dangerous ideas leading to serious harm, especially as sexual asphyxiation could lead to cardiac arrest and coma. Leave any such risky notions to imagination and please yourself in a safe manner!

Breast cancer arises when healthy cells of breast tissue alter and may begin to grow out of control which might look as a lump inside breast tissue. Breast Cancer Treatment involves chemotherapy, radiotherapy,surgery according on the kind of cancer.

Phimosis: Causes, Symptoms, and Treatment
Phimosis is a health condition in which the foreskin is not retracted or drawn back from around the tip of the penis.

Does masturbating hurt your kidneys?
There's no proof that masturbating adversely influences your kidney health. There's also no proof that masturbating may cause:

renal failure
renal disease
kidney pain
Some individuals wrongly assume that a loss of protein and nutrients via semen might lead to kidney impairment. Again, there's no scientific foundation for this claim.

There are extremely few nutrients in semen that are present to feed sperm. The few nutrients don't have a big influence on your health.

One 2013 research review

Trusted Source revealed that there's an average of 5.04 grams of protein in 100 milliliters of semen, or the equivalent of around 0.25 grams in one ejaculation of semen.

To restore this quantity of protein, you would only need to drink roughly 1/2 tablespoon of milkTrusted Source or consume 0.1 ouncesTrusted Source of chickpeas.

Masturbation and kidney stones
There's some evidence that masturbating may assist clear kidney stones. In a 2020 study, researchers studied the impact of masturbating 3 to 4 times per week for dropping 5- to 10-millimeter stones.

The researchers discovered that masturbating paired with normal medical treatment was equally beneficial as taking the drug tamsulosin along with regular medical therapy. Though the study presents a fascinating hypothesis, it needs additional investigation to properly grasp.

What are the advantages of masturbation?
There are a limited number of research especially looking at the advantages of masturbating. Most study has focused at the advantages of orgasms or ejaculation.

However, masturbating releases hormones and substances such as:

dopamine\sendorphins\soxytocin
testosterone\sprolactin
Changes in these hormone levels might possibly have advantages such as:

boosting your mood
alleviating stress and anxiety
promoting tranquility
helping you fall asleep
For those with vaginas, masturbation may also help ease period cramps.

Ejaculation and prostate cancer risk
In a 2016 study, researchers identified a negative link between ejaculation frequency and the chance of acquiring prostate cancer.

The researchers observed that those who ejaculated more than 21 times per month were less likely to have had prostate cancer after a 10-year follow up than people who ejaculated 4 to 7 times.

However, it's important emphasizing that correlation doesn't equal causation. More study is required to properly understand the relationship between ejaculation frequency and prostate cancer risk.

Are there any probable adverse effects of masturbation?
Masturbation itself isn't known to produce any health issues. However, there are some possible physical and mental adverse effects.

Guilt

Many individuals sense guilt after masturbating, frequently because of their religious, cultural, or spiritual convictions.

Masturbation is a natural and healthy sexual behavior and there's no reason to feel embarrassed about it. If you're feeling guilty about masturbating, you may find it beneficial to speak to someone you trust or a therapist specialized in sexual health.

Addiction

A masturbation addiction refers to the urge to masturbate uncontrollably. There's no scientific diagnostic for masturbation addiction, and there's still dispute whether it should be categorized as an addiction or a compulsion.

Signs that you may have acquired harmful masturbation practices include:

masturbation interferes with your everyday life\syou find it difficult to quit thinking about masturbating\syou masturbate even when you aren't aroused\syou masturbate in public\smasturbating adversely influences your relationships or social life\syou use masturbation to cope with bad feelings
you cancel plans or activities to masturbate
Some individuals able to cope with masturbation addiction on their own, but many people also benefit from meeting with a sex therapist.

Physical side effects
For a person with a penis, it's claimed that masturbating with an abnormally firm grip will desensitize your nerves and lessen sensation. This illness is termed "death grip syndrome."

Over time, this may make it impossible to orgasm without recreating the same movements.

People with vaginas might also have a similar problem where your nerves get desensitized from masturbating with high pressure.

If you're suffering desensitization, you may benefit from taking a vacation from masturbating for a few weeks or adjusting your technique to utilize less pressure.

Frequent masturbation might also contribute to pain or chafing. If this occurs to you, you might consider taking a pause until the soreness lessens. Using lubricant while masturbating may avoid the problem from recurring.

What might cause pain in your kidneys after masturbation?
It's quite improbable that masturbating would create discomfort in your kidneys. If you're having discomfort in your lower back after masturbating, it's extremely probable

that the ache is caused by bad posture during masturbating.

You may treat this discomfort with a hot pack and nonsteroidal anti-inflammatory medicine.

Another option is that you're coincidentally also struggling with kidney stones or another renal condition and didn't realize until after you masturbated.

If you don't follow appropriate hygiene habits while masturbating, it's conceivable that you might acquire a urinary tract infection (UTI) (UTI). Persons with vaginas are far more prone than people with penises to have a UTI because they have a shorter urethra.

Symptoms of a UTI include:

burning when urinating

frequent desire to urinate\sabdominal pain\sfoul-smelling urine\scloudy pee\sblood in your urine

If left untreated, UTIs can spread to your kidneys. A kidney infection is a potentially dangerous illness that needs quick medical care. Along with the symptoms of a bladder infection, it may cause:

fever\ssharp ache in your lower back nausea\svomiting\schills

If you're coping with any form of worrisome discomfort after masturbating, it's a good idea to get medical help as soon as possible for thorough assessment and treatment.